the twilight saga
breaking dawn
part 2

ISBN 978-1-4803-2432-9

HAL•LEONARD®
CORPORATION
7777 W. BLUEMOUND RD. P.O. BOX 13819 MILWAUKEE, WI 53213

In Australia Contact:
Hal Leonard Australia Pty. Ltd.
4 Lentara Court
Cheltenham, Victoria, 3192 Australia
Email: ausadmin@halleonard.com.au

Visit Hal Leonard Online at
www.halleonard.com

TWILIGHT OVERTURE

Composed by
CARTER BURWELL

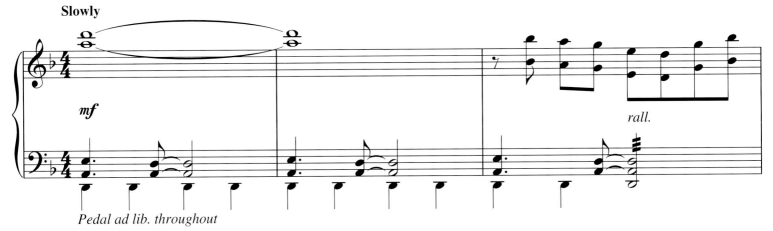

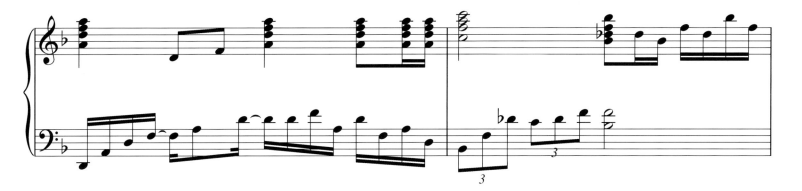

Moderately fast

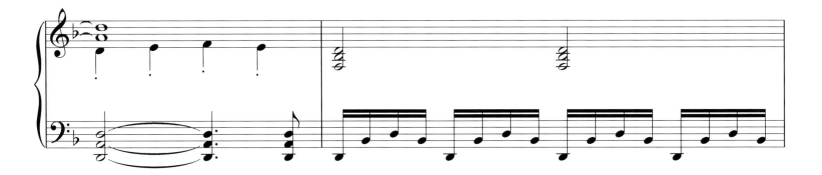

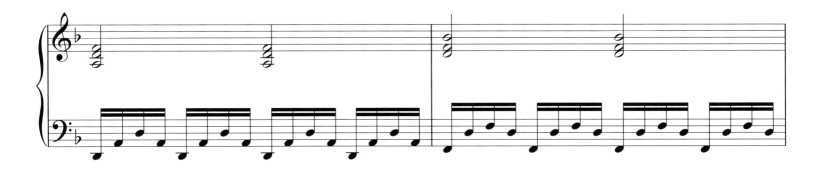

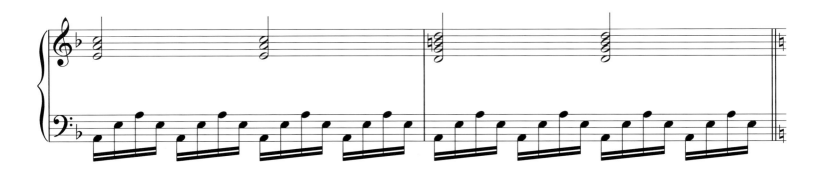

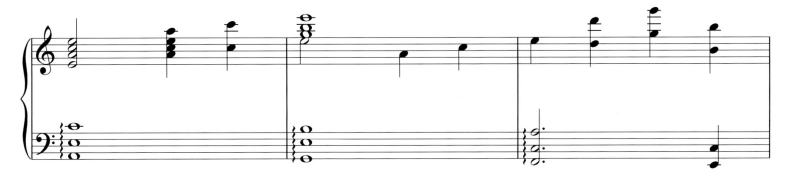

Moderately

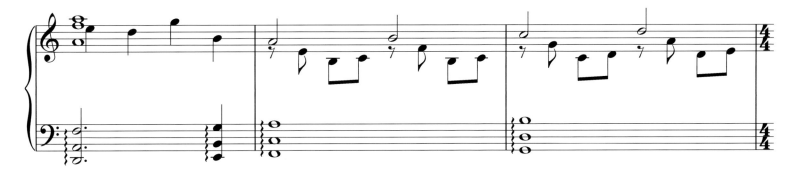

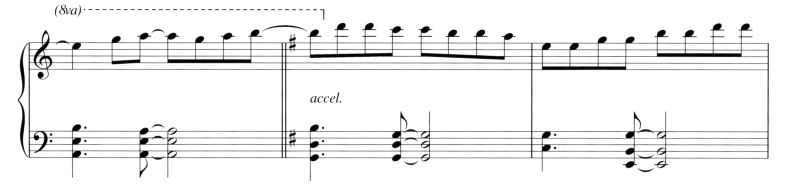

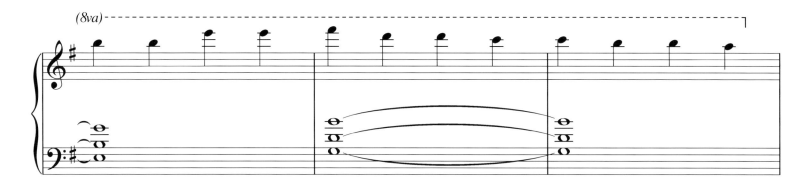

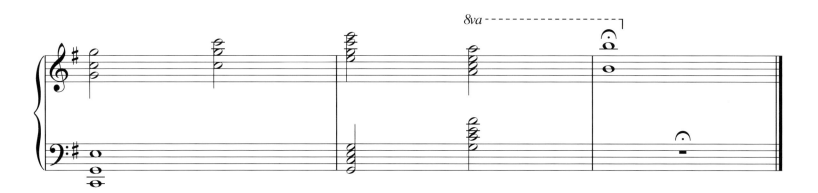

A WORLD BRIGHT AND BUZZING

Composed by
CARTER BURWELL

Moderately fast

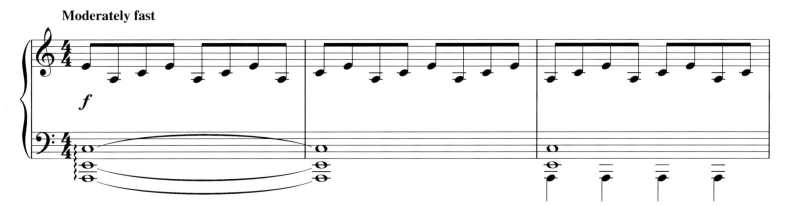

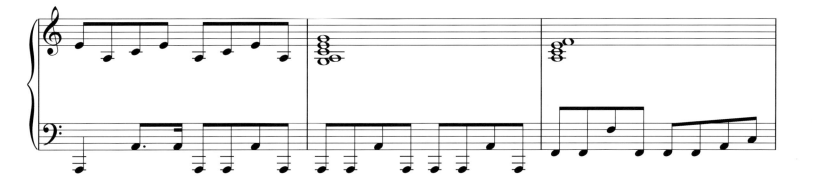

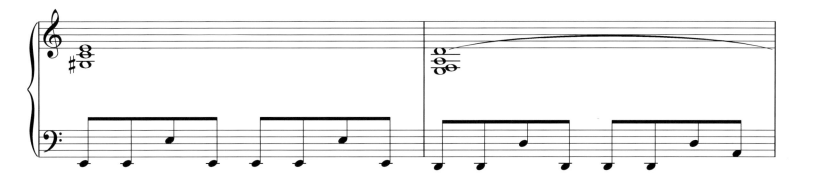

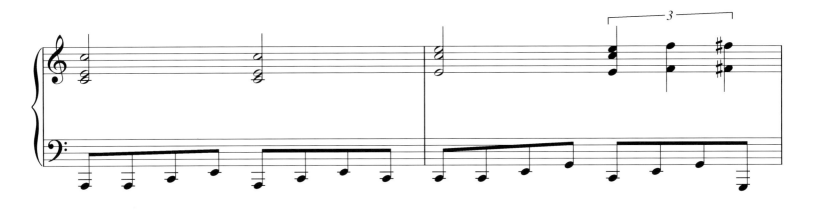

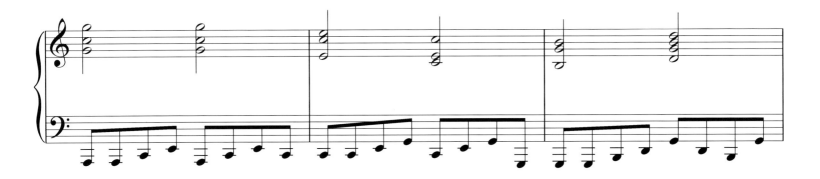

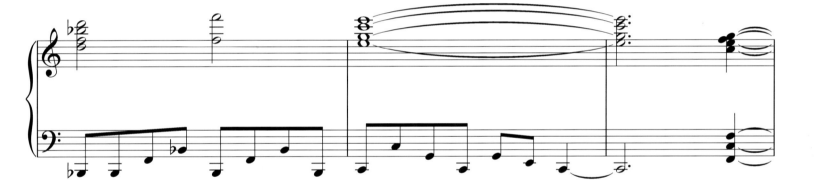

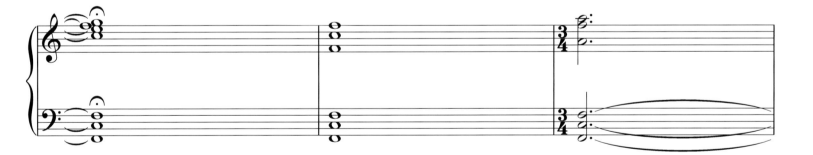

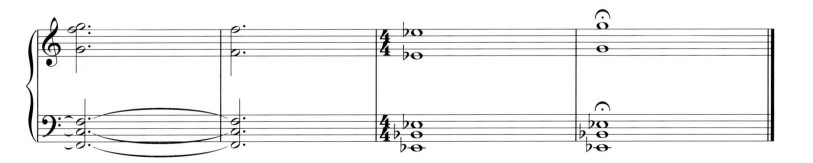

CATCHING SNOWFLAKES

Composed by
CARTER BURWELL

Moderately

Pedal ad lib. throughout

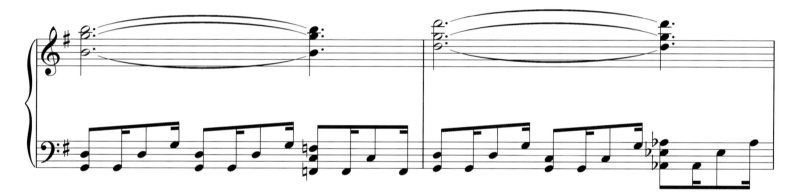

RENESMEE'S LULLABY/
SOMETHING TERRIBLE

Composed by
CARTER BURWELL

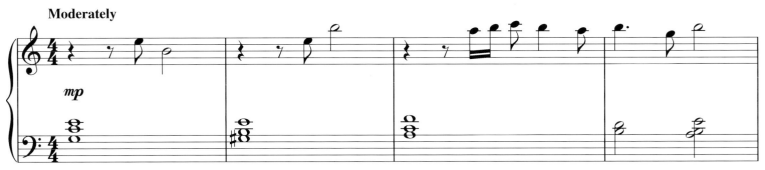

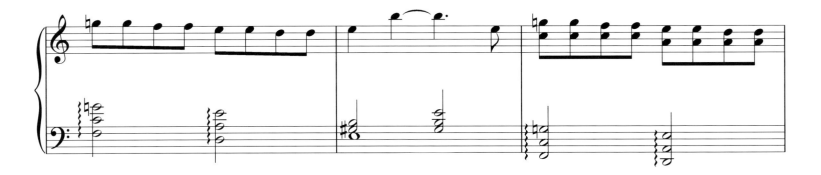

molto rit.

8vb

MEET RENESMEE

Composed by
CARTER BURWELL

Moderately

mp

Pedal ad lib. throughout

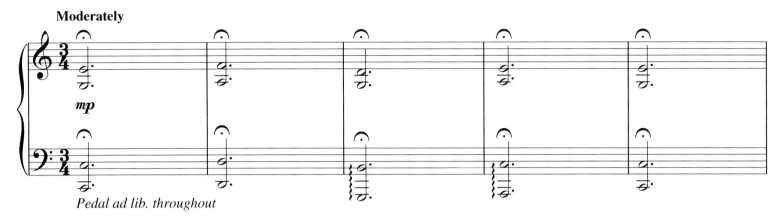

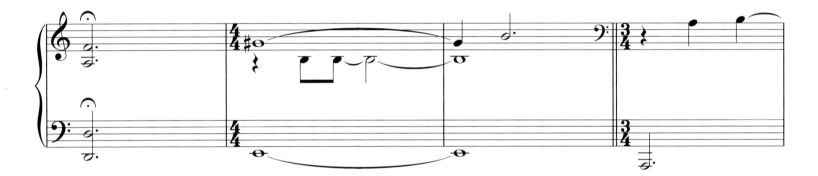

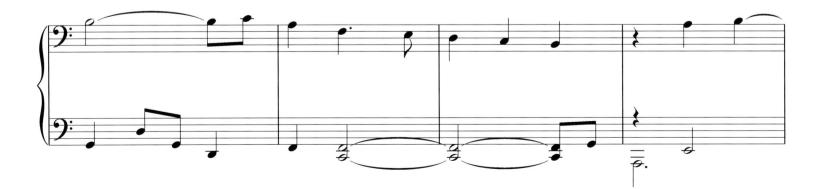

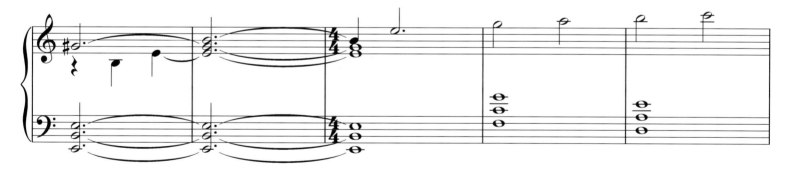

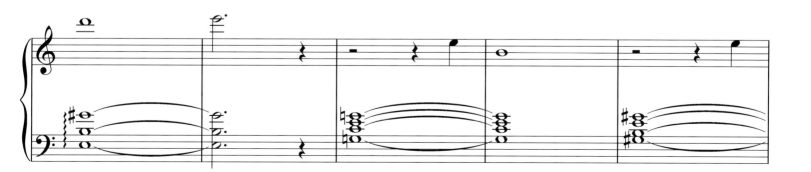

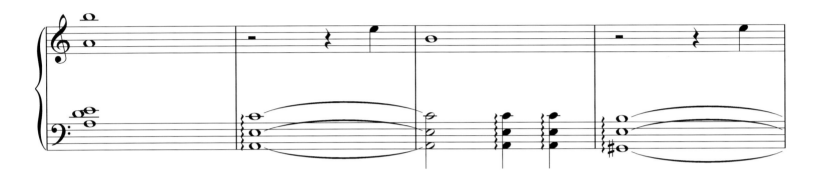

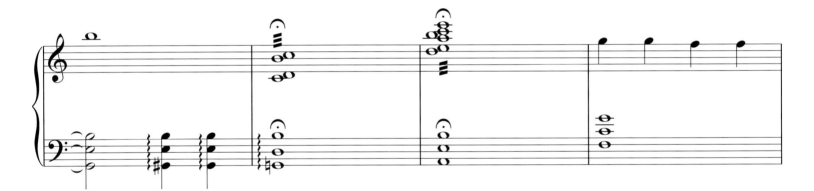

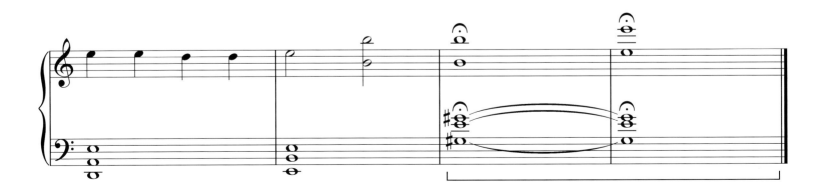

A WAY WITH THE WORLD

Composed by
CARTER BURWELL

Moderately, expressively

mp

Pedal ad lib. throughout

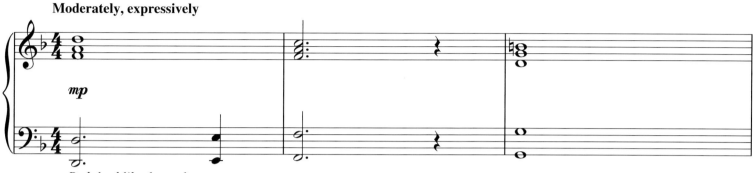

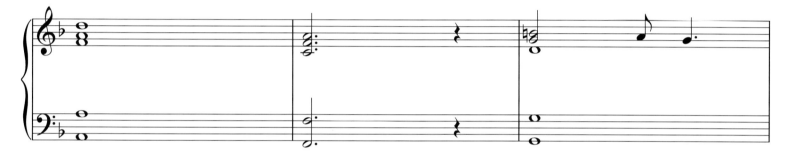

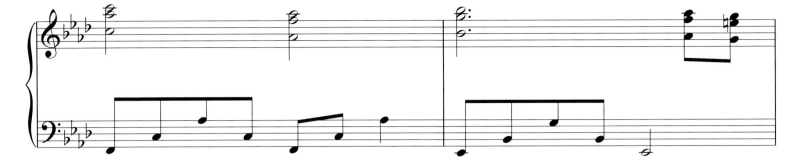

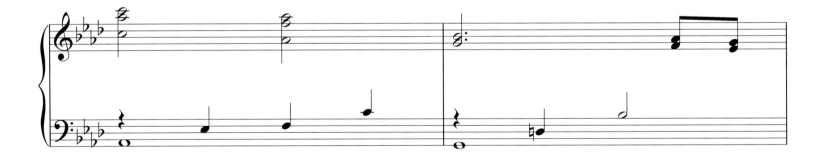

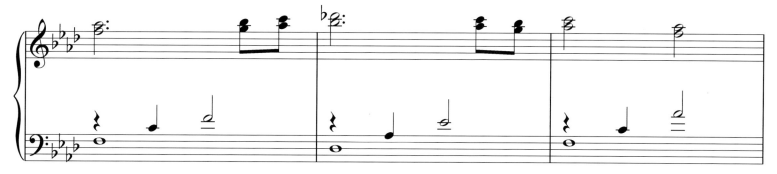

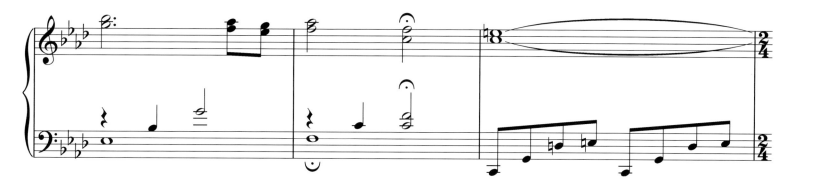

PRESENT TIME

Composed by
CARTER BURWELL

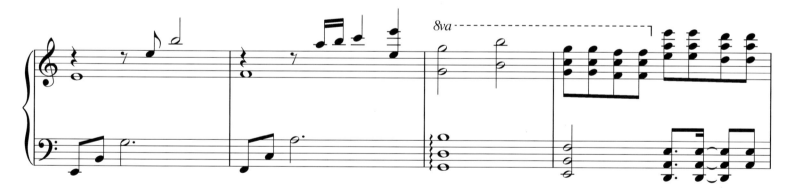

AT BEDTIME A CHILD ASKS ABOUT DEATH

Composed by
CARTER BURWELL

Slowly, very expressively

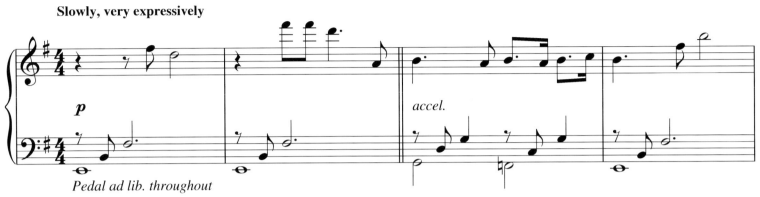

Pedal ad lib. throughout

Slightly faster

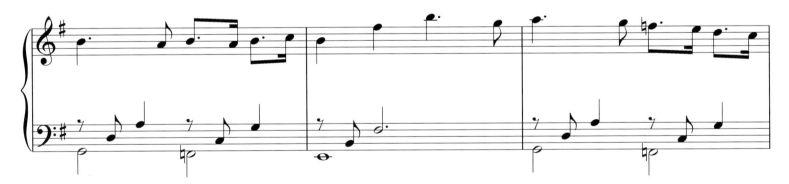

THIS EXTRAORDINARY LIFE

Composed by
CARTER BURWELL

Moderately

mp

Pedal ad lib. throughout

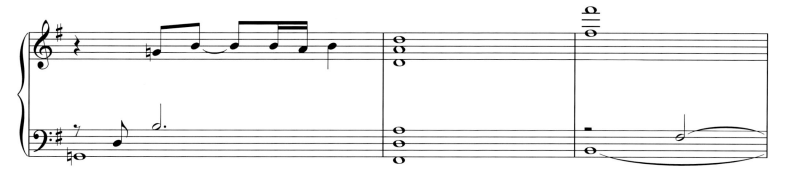

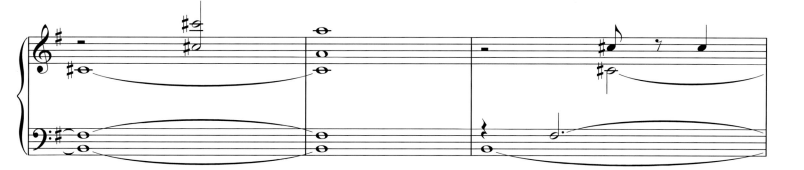

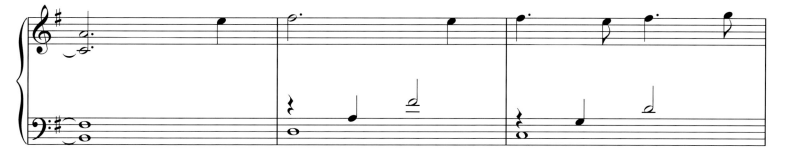

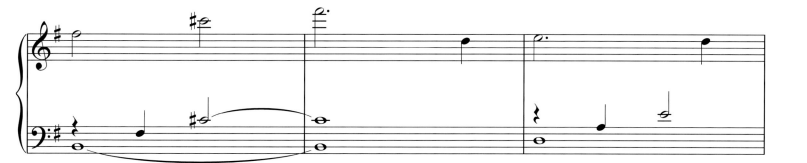

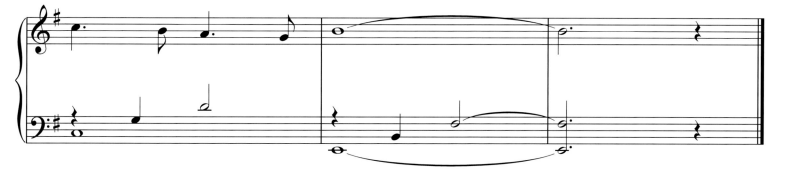

SUCH A PRIZE

Composed by
CARTER BURWELL

Moderately

mf

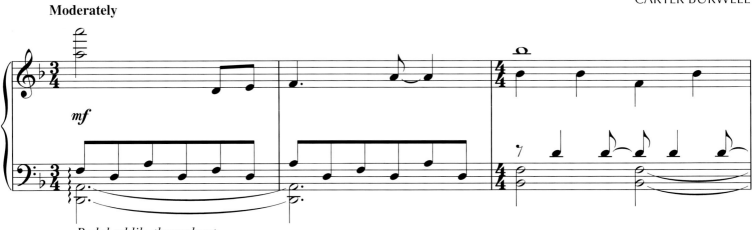

Pedal ad lib. throughout

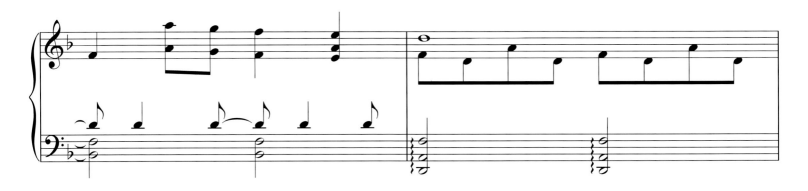

8vb

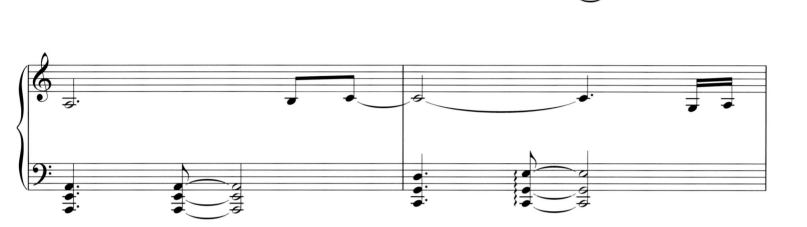